Be A Better Builder

Be A Better Builder

AN ESSENTIAL GUIDE FOR RESIDENTIAL CONTRACTORS

Ron Benhart

iUniverse

BE A BETTER BUILDER
AN ESSENTIAL GUIDE FOR RESIDENTIAL CONTRACTORS

iUniverse books may be ordered through booksellers or by contacting:

iUniverse
1663 Liberty Drive
Bloomington, IN 47403
www.iuniverse.com
844-349-9409

ISBN: 978-1-6632-1262-7 (sc)
ISBN: 978-1-6632-1263-4 (e)

Print information available on the last page.

iUniverse rev. date: 10/29/2020

TABLE OF CONTENTS

SECTION 1: OPENING REMARKS

HISTORY

In 1952, Bill Benhart started a residential construction business in the suburbs of Chicago. In 1958, he moved the business to Pinellas County Florida and built a marina. He sold the marina after two years to concentrate on the construction business. He also became the developer of a 300 lot subdivision. In 1970 he developed a 24 lot subdivision.

By 1971 my brother Marvin and I joined the business. Business was good. In a 2 ½ year period we completed 84 custom homes before our father was totally disabled by a stroke. Marvin and I continued and developed another 15 lot subdivision in 1980.

In 1985 we discovered North Carolina. Over the next 4 years we built out our Florida Lot inventory and developed a 35 lot subdivision in Haywood County NC. When we left Florida permanently in 1989, we had completed over 400 custom homes.

In the mid 1990's we were joined by my grandson, Jason Revelia. He learned the development process in 1998 when we developed our last 32 lot subdivision where he lives today. This continued tradition started in Florida and required at least one of the business principals to live in every development we under took. This decision was cited by many clients as a factor they considered when deciding to utilize us as a general contractor.

One huge advantage we had for the first 45 years of the business was my mother. She handled all office and financial matters and knew as much or more about the construction business as most general contractors. When she retired my daughter Melissa assumed her duties and performed as well.

Over the years we received recognition as best building contractor, senior friendly business, and developer. We also received numerous letters from happy clients. The best recognition we had came from Bob and Sandy Brantly who still reside in the house we built for them in Maggie Valley. They are as happy with their house today as they were when they wrote us in 2007. I quote from their letter:

"Sandy and I have been in our new home here in Maggie Valley for over a month. I wanted to be in it awhile before I wrote this letter, so I could discover all the little problems which are usually inherent in any new home. However, try as I may, I can find none!"

"To be able to occupy a new house and not have a "punch list" of problems needing remedy is unheard of in our experience. I should have expected no less, however, as from the beginning, we have had nothing but a positive working relationship. You are truly professional in your trade, in every sense of the word."

1

SAFETY MATTERS

One topic not discussed in the body of this book is often given a low priority by many general contractors. That topic is safety. It is imperative that general contractors insist on having a safety plan that requires safe work practices, protective clothing and equipment, and complete cooperation of all tradesmen involved. Ban the use of alcohol and drugs during working hours. Limit access for interested bystanders -especially children- during working hours. Hold regular safety meetings. Post emergency phone numbers including the power supplier on the inside of the port-o-let door. All tradesmen and your insurance company will thank you.

TRAITS OF A BETTER BUILDER

When any building (a house, for our purposes) is constructed, the central figure is the general contractor. The general contractor must be knowledgeable, honest, capable, a good manager, and able to interact with all types of people. He has to coordinate the efforts of building and zoning officials, inspectors, Architects/Designers, Mortgage Officers, Engineers, Surveyors, Suppliers, Subcontractors, Homeowner's Associations, and employees to reach an objective – producing a code compliant finished product for a satisfied client in a reasonable time period.

A Better Builder's Individual Goals are:
1. Build good relationships with all parties involved.
2. Provide a cordial job atmosphere where everyone wants to work with and FOR you.
3. Promote repeat business because he is knowledgeable, organized, personable, efficient, and produces superior results.

PRELIMINARY CHECKLIST

General contractors will need to address the following items before starting any project:

1. Make sure you have a valid contractor's license for the proposed project (make sure license covers the cost of the project).
2. Purchase general liability, blanket workman's compensation and builders risk insurance policies that will cover the project.
3. A Lawyer who has reviewed your contract, change order forms, and insurance coverages.
4. A Surveyor.
5. A Geotechnical engineer you can use to address soil problems you may encounter.
6. A Structural engineer.
7. A Home designer or Architect.
8. A comfortable understanding of basic mathematics and geometry.
9. Basic accounting knowledge and a good CPA.
10. Adequate working capital-(minimum of $50,000).
11. A knowledge and understanding of construction financing, mortgages, and draw schedules.
12. Completely filled out specifications for the project.
13. Well and septic installers if project calls for one or both (Know the State requirements for both).
14. Suppliers with active accounts; know their delivery details and payment policies.
15. The knowledge to take off your own materials for a project.
16. Secure copies of your subcontractor's insurance coverage. Know their payment terms and work practices.

SECTION 2:   RELATIONSHIPS

Remember the basic rule of business -- you treat people the way you want to be treated and expect the same in return. The vast majority of people will respond positively and everyone's role is simplified.

As a general contractor you will work with the following groups of people:

PLAN PROVIDERS

House Plans can be obtained from:
1. Prospective Clients,
2. Design Contractors,
3. Internet Plan Service Companies,
4. Houses you have built,
5. Local Home Designers, and
6. Architects.

The best course of action to follow is to work with a home designer who will provide a plan addressing the client's wishes and who can modify any plan or sketch you or the client provides.

LENDERS

All lenders have essentially the same requirements. Some are easier to work with than others. After dealing with multiple lenders select the one you have found easiest to work with. Cultivate this relationship and refer clients to this lender. As long as you are a better builder and the client qualifies for a mortgage you will have few if any issues with the lender.

PERMITTING AND INSPECTION AGENCIES

There is virtually no negotiating latitude with this group of people. They enforce the building code and state laws. Ask about their permitting requirements and inspection practices. Be sure to be at the building site when inspections are to be performed to get first hand any changes that needs to be made. By doing their job inspectors are ensuring you follow the code and thereby reduce or eliminate costly mistakes. Remember to allow a full day for all inspections after the inside work has been roughed in. The inspector should have a clean job inside and outside to perform inspections. The only work being done should be outside during inspections.

When applying for a permit, take the following items:

1. Complete set of house plans including foundation plan, floor plan, elevations and wall section
2. Completed set of specifications
3. Well permit or water tap fee paid
4. Septic permit or sewer tap fee paid
5. Address and legal description of building site; obtain address at addressing office.
6. A contract with the client
7. Survey if available

If applying for a permit for the first time at any permit office, add a copy of your license and copies of your insurance coverages to the above list. This makes a great first impression and demonstrates you are fully prepared to do the job.

SUPPLIERS AND VENDORS

The key for dealing with these people is knowing what you want and when you want it. After securing the permit alert the various suppliers of your proposed schedule and items needed. Determine the lead time for deliveries. Ask about billing schedules and payment due dates. If you need floor or roof trusses, discuss this with the manufacturer.

Any scarce or seldom used items, such as a special cast iron tub, glulam beam, or clay roof tiles may need to be ordered immediately. During Boom times in the construction business you should probably check on such items before the contract with the client has been signed.

Give the supplier tentative delivery dates and keep them informed of your progress or lack thereof. Continued communication will ensure you receive the items when you need them. If you pay your bills on time and order appropriately, suppliers will want your business.

SUBCONTRACTORS

Our time-tested formula for dealing with subcontractors works fantastically All subs are given 7 to 10 working days' notice of when their services are needed. We ask how long it will take them to do their job. We give them these days with no clutter and no other sub working inside at the same time. When they are done, they are paid with the understanding that if something needs attention, they will address it by the next day after it is discovered. All subs we have used over the years like this practice. If the general contractor checks on them every day they are on the project, we find virtually no problems with their work. This also leads to not having confrontations between the different subs while on the project. We also require each sub to clean up after themselves daily and when their work is completed.

Any special items required for the subs such as a tub or shower unit needs to be on site when they start their work. Schedule appropriately.

Money, easy access, and an organized work environment, can be powerful motivators. If the general contractor cannot pay a sub when he finishes his work, at the very least tell them when payment will be made and keep your word.

By using this system, we have had many of the same subs for over 25 years. Remember, when a sub completes his work when he said he would and does it for the quoted price there are no surprises. You need to continue using this sub. Even though a general contractor is in charge of a project, it really is a partnership and their work is a reflection on you. Long term relationships really do matter.

PROSPECTS AND CLIENTS

Remember the basic rules:

1. Treat all clients and prospects the way you want to be treated.
2. Keep them informed.
3. Be totally honest.
4. If an issue arises and you are unsure of the correct answer, say you need to research it. Do the research and get the correct answer, and communicate it to the client as soon as possible. No delays!

Review plans, specifications, and contract with clients completely before signing them. Have the client initial each page that does not require a signature as you go over it with them. Have them sign a blueprint and keep this copy in your file. Do not give it to any subcontractor or supplier.

If clients bring you a complete set of plans but say change this and this, have the plans redrawn to incorporate the changes to avoid confusion and liability. Only if the changes are VERY MINOR would we alter an existing plan to conform to their wishes.

Meet the clients at least once a month on the job site. Review the progress, answer their questions, and get your questions answered.

After you have started construction and the client wants to make changes (they will), make sure to complete a change order form detailing the changes and the costs involved. After they sign give them a copy and put the original in your file for future reference. Specify when the additional money is to be paid.

After framing is completed but before the plumber, electrician, heating/air, and gas contractors start their work, schedule a walk through with the client. Have all the cabinets and vanities located on the floor. Also locate the toilets, water heater, washer and dryer, and any special features. Discuss locations for electric receptacles, switches, lights, phones, television, internet, heating/cooling vents, and return air. Consider using a master control box by the meter base, electrical panel or in a utility room, where telephone, television, and internet lines can be run to the exterior. Also consider running a second line for each service to the exterior, crawl space, or garage in the event a wire is damaged.

Copies of client selection sheets are included in Section 9. Give clients selection sheet #1 when the contract is signed, or the footing is poured. Selection sheets #2 should be given to clients when the walk-thru after framing is conducted. Selection sheet #3 should be given to the client when the painter starts work. Do NOT give clients all the sheets at once unless you want to be bombarded with questions and changes.

Each time you receive a selection sheet from a client, confirm that these are their final choices. Explain that changes can be made after the specific items have been ordered or installed but at additional cost and risk of delaying completion of the job.

When you have completed the job and a problem develops you probably have the obligation to correct it. Find the solution and correct the problem promptly and be cordial while doing it. The solution costs you time and money but that is the price you pay for being in business. Your reputation is at stake.

Some potential clients can be trouble. During the process of discussing the project with a potential client we had a rule. At least two of our company principals had to agree we could do the job without having an adversarial relationship develop. If we decided we did not want the job we never told the prospect. We would tell them it would be at least a year before we could start their job. With especially troublesome prospects we figured the approximate price and doubled it. When we quoted it to the prospect, they got the message and we parted ways. Sometimes your best job is the one you did not get.

Another situation that can arise involves a prospect that you quoted a price, but he opted to use a competitor. Something happened that resulted in the prospect being unhappy with the competitor and he returns to ask you for help, sometimes asking if you will take over and complete his job. The few times this has happened our answer was always the same: thanks, but no thanks. He was obviously unhappy and the possible negative results are simply too great, not even considering the legal aspects involved.

Two notes of caution:

First, include as standard features the following: garage door operators and the accompanying low voltage wiring; heat-vent-lights in all bathrooms; garbage disposal wiring in all kitchens (even if it will not be used); vent fans in utility rooms; gutter guard; insulated garage doors. Offer to install the client's mail box if he provides one.

Second, when specifying allowance values do not lowball them. Use mid-grade brand names for cabinets, appliances, fixtures, and flooring when determining the amounts allowed. Let the clients decide how they want to spend their money. Be realistic.

As a contractor your ultimate goal is satisfied customers. When you walk into a store or restaurant and meet a previous customer who is cordial and states he or she is happy with the job you did for him or her you can compliment yourself. You know you did your job the right way. Clients like this are your best advertising and it is FREE!

SECTION 3:   SCHEDULING

Proper scheduling is a must. It will ensure the project moves forward with minimal conflicts and lost time. The construction sequence included in this book is NOT A ONE SIZE FITS ALL OUTLINE. You may have to make adjustments due to some characteristics of a particular job, the weather, material shortages, or countless other conditions. But the closer you follow the sequence the better and faster your results will be. Some important steps are as follows:

1. Keep everyone informed if modifications affect their trade or materials.
2. Get the well done (if required) prior to doing the concrete and masonry. This will ensure you have water. There is nothing worse than finding out water is not available when the home is being framed or later in the process.
3. Make sure temporary power is installed while working on the foundation. Contract the electric provider when you start your work to allow for line construction if it is required.
4. Be sure drive and culverts are roughed in prior to concrete delivery. Rough grade before framing commences so materials can be place where they are needed and there are no obstacles for the framers.
5. Schedule material deliveries so each sub has what he needs when he starts.
6. When framing is fully completed on the inside your subcontractors work in the following order:

1. Plumber
2. Heating/Air contractor
3. Electrician
4. Gas contractor

Let each sub finish his work before the next sub begins. Follow this same order when they return to finish the job.

SECTION 4:   SPECIFIC REMCOMMENDATIONS BY TRADE

CONCRETE AND MASONRY

You have one chance to do a foundation right. DO NOT CUT CORNERS. Repairs necessitated by mistake are both time consuming and costly. Do it right the first time. Take off your own materials. Use batter boards. Consider removing any trees within 15 feet of the structure (consult client). Have all utilities located prior to beginning any work. Get any required surveying completed before beginning and include the establishment of a benchmark if the site is in a flood zone. Should you encounter soft soils or excessive fill contact your geotechnical engineer.

After scraping the house site and removing grass and any excess soil locate the drive, septic, and well location. Be sure the proposed house site meets all setbacks and restrictions. Locate retaining walls if necessary. Make sure your batterboards are square. Locate entry points for water and waste lines. Can they go through the block or must they go under the footer? Consider sleeves for any under footing utility lines. Check all footing and pad locations to be sure they are correct.

Now you are ready to dig, place your rebar, and pour your footing.

After the footing is poured recheck EVERYTHING (all locations, dimensions, placement, and batter board heights). Be totally correct before doing blockwork or poured walls.

When placing your footing rebars install a vertical #5 rebar at each inside and outside corner that is centered to go in the block cavity if you are using concrete block walls. Lap 40 diameters to the footing rebars. Use open bottom bond beam block for the top course, reinforce with a #5 rebar overlapping continuously. Pour concrete in each vertical cavity with a rebar as well as the top course of block creating a tie beam. Insert proper length of ½" anchor bolts into the concrete as you pour every 48" on center to secure the PT plates. This is insurance to strengthen the entire foundation.

Verify finish wall heights while the mason is working.

When placing material orders be sure to order enough of each item to have a few leftover. Order enough concrete to ensure you have little left when each pour is completed. Remember to add concrete for step downs in the footing.

If using a poured reinforced wall remember to insert sleeves in the wall for any gas, water, sewer, electrical and AC lines at the proper locations. Insert 8"x16" wood forms in the wall at appropriate locations for foundation vents in a crawl space.

Check with your pest control company for how they intend to treat for termites before pouring footings and slabs. Use 4" expansion joint against concrete and masonry walls before pouring slabs.

After masonry walls are complete do any required or necessary waterproofing, foundation drains, and possibly gutter drains and have them inspected. Then backfill.

In a crawlspace project have a vapor barrier installed when the building is insulated and all work below the wood floor has been completed. Store extra roof shingles, vinyl siding, drip edge, etc. atop the crawl space vapor barrier (no wood).

Wait one year after the house is completed to install concrete or asphalt drives to account for settling.

FRAMING

Take off your materials yourself – only you know how you frame. Order materials by load with notations what each item is used for. Give the framer a copy. Do not order the entire framing package at one time. Order loads as needed. Cover orders from the elements when delivered and each night.

Verify all rough openings for windows and doors with the supplier. Make sure your framer has and understands all the rough openings including interior door heights with finished floor installed. When framing the openings for exterior windows and doors, leave the openings 2 inches larger in both directions to allow for uncompacted insulation to be installed between the dimension lumber and window or door frame. Extend sheeting at a minimum 3" into each door and window opening. Cover all wood exterior walls with a quality house wrap. Cut finish opening to fit when installing the window or door with the house wrap between the sheeting and the window or door frame. Use Tyvek tape or a exterior insulation tape to cover the joint where the window or door meets the house wrap. The house wrap should extend over all flashings where a roof meets a wall and a wall meets a floor.

Be sure framer understands how to build stairs using dresser boards. See the detail in the "Drawings" section 9.

Glue and nail or screw floor sheeting to joists or trusses.

Use all ground contact pressure treated lumber. Use pressure treated risers for all exterior doors with 4"x4" 90-degree galvanized flashing. See drawing enclosed.

Use 6" exterior walls with studs 16" on center and r-19 insulation. IF garage is to be finished with drywall and trim use 6" walls and insulate walls and ceilings.

Use solid sheeting (plywood or OSB) and not foam on exterior walls.

Use a minimum 30# felt or peel and stick to dry in roof immediately after sheeting is completed. If sheeting is not completed and rain or snow is expected dry in the sheeting that is completed. Be sure to check for adequate sheeting nailing before nailing the dry in.

Provide an opening for drywall delivery on the second floor. Leave a window out if necessary until the drywall is delivered. If you have a double hung fire escape window remove both sashes and be careful.

Have roof shingles delivered on a boom truck and require the framer to unload them after the roof is dried in.

Bridge joists 8' and longer.

Strip truss ceiling with 1x3 spruce 16" on center.

Use hurricane clips on all roof rafters and trusses.

If using vinyl siding and there are penetrations for AC disconnects, hose bibs, electric receptacles, or gas lines, mount a stained cedar block 6"x6" or 6"x10" atop the house wrap and butt the vinyl siding to it. Have the plumber, electrician, or gas mechanic mount his equipment on the block. This will prevent siding defects such as bubbles or compressions. AC disconnects generally require the 6"x10" size.

Install towel bar deadwood in baths.

Provide outriggers for mantles at fireplaces if needed.

Use dresser boards on all stairways. See drawing enclosed in Section 9.

Install curtain rod deadwood at the upper corners of each window and door and in the center of any opening 60" or more in length.

In garages install deadwood for overhead door tracks and automatic openers. Consult the door provider for proper location.

Install cabinet deadwood at heights of 6' 9" to 7' above the floor and 32 ½" to 36" above the floor on walls where kitchen cabinets are to be mounted. In bathrooms mount deadwood for vanities at 27" to 30 ½" above the floor. If 36" tall vanities are used, set the deadwood at 32 ½" to 36" above the floor.

If stone tops are to be used in the kitchen or on free standing islands, contact the floor truss provider or your structural engineer if joists are involved to see if any reinforcement of floor system is required.

DECK AND PORCH FLOORS

Common exterior floors are:

Pressure treated lumber. Use all ground contact material. It is worth the extra cost.

Trex or similar composites. Available at increased cost and with specific fastening requirements this material may well be worth the money, especially on uncovered decks.

Concrete – good all-around choice if the site permits its use. Remember to clean off caulk, drywall spackle, and paint before turning the house over to the owners. Clean the garage floor also.

Tile – Not a good choice where snow, ice, and freezing temperatures are common.

FIREPLACES AND CHIMNEYS

All masonry fireplaces are costly while prefab units are more cost efficient. Prefab gas units can be used without a chimney as long as it is not in a bedroom and gas logs are used. Prefab chimneys are readily available if wood is the preferred fuel. If using a prefab unit be sure to follow the manufacturer's instructions, especially regarding insulation.

Masonry chimneys present unique flashing problems. Discuss this with the mason involved and secure the pre-bent shapes you will use before the mason starts work above the existing roof.

Basic rules for chimneys are:

1. No chimney in roof valleys.
2. Use a cricket on the highest part of the roof above the chimney.
3. Start flashing at the lowest part of the roof where the chimney exits the roof and proceed to the highest point where the cricket is.
4. Rough in a gas line to the firebox if gas is ever to be used as fuel.
5. When finishing frame chimneys and stucco or stone veneer on masonry chimneys keep the siding, stucco, or veneer a minimum of 1" above the finished roof surface to allow shingles to be replaced and water to flow. Finish stucco, brick, and stone veneer on chimneys before permanent roof is applied. A fabricated metal cap should extend over the veneer, brick, or stucco at least 2".
6. If stone veneer is to meet wood flooring in front of a hearth use a ground 1/8" thicker than the wood flooring. This will allow the stone mason to lay the rock on top of the ground. Remove the ground when the mortar has dried, you can then slide the wood flooring under the stone. See attached drawing in Section #9.

ROOFING

Common roofing materials are shingles and metal roofing. Others available are tile, shakes, and tar & gravel. If you use anything other than shingles, be sure to use a roofer that is both knowledgeable and experienced in the system utilized.

General rules are:
1. Check the dry in after the plumber and electricians work to be sure penetrations for electrical risers, vents, and plumbing stacks are waterproof.
2. Use 16" metal flashings in all valleys.
3. Always use drip edge.
4. Flash barge rafters where they rest on roof.

EXTERIOR FINISH

Typical exterior finishes are aluminum and vinyl siding, individual wood boards, ply wood sheets, cement boards, cement sheets, stone, and brick. Aluminum dents. Anything wood or cement requires refinishing unless it is 1 x 8 and 1 x 4 pressure treated used as board and batten allowed to weather. Stone and brick are expensive. We found the best overall alternative to be:

1 x cedar fascia and birdboxes primed on all sides before installation, aluminum or vinyl soffit, vinyl siding and some stone or vinyl accents. Crawl space foundations were left stuccoed and unpainted if they were block. Poured walls were not stuccoed or painted. The only maintenance required is pressure cleaning every 3 to 5 years and re-staining the fascia. Remember to keep whatever siding you use at least 1" above deck and porch floors and finish roofing materials to allow for easier maintenance and/or replacement.

INSULATION

Before insulating any building, be sure to check all walls for straightness. Crooked, warped, or twisted studs lead to bulges or depressions in the wall. Use a 6 foot level or straight edge to check the walls. Pay special attention to kitchens and baths where cabinets and vanities will go. Cut and shim, plane, and add scabs as required to ensure a straight wall.

Use fiberglass batts and not cellulose. The best attic insulation is a batt with blown fiberglass on top to get the total R value needed.

For masonry walls use 4' x 8' foil covered foam sheets. Place 1"x 2" or 1" x 3" treated wood strips 16" on center and use hard nails to fasten the wood to the concrete or block behind the foam panels. Cover with drywall. An alternate method is to frame a 4" wall and mount it .1/2 " away from the concrete or block, install batts, then install drywall.

PAINTING - INSIDE

Before the painter arrives inspect, strip, label and stack all trim. Provide sawhorses or scaffold frames to stack trim material after it receives the first coat. Stain and clear coat or prime all trim prior to installation. Give them plenty of room to work. Do the inside painting first. No other tradesman should be working inside while the painters are working.

Have all materials on hand when the painter arrives. Include a box of rags. Be sure drop cloths cover all concrete floors.

After all other trades have finished inside have the painter touch up and apply any finished coats required.

PAINTING – OUTSIDE

Apply second coat of stain to fascia and birdboxes after the framers install them. Wood siding should be primed on all sides before installation. Exterior doors and wood siding are the final painting steps outside. Cover decks and porch floors with drop cloths. Leave stucco unpainted.

If you use pressure treated lumber for porch flooring, railings, steps, posts, and beams do not paint or stain for 1 year. Let it dry completely. We recommend not painting or staining pressure treated lumber at all. It is too maintenance intensive and requires frequent pressure cleaning and refinishing. If a client wants it finished, we recommend oil stain and not paint because paint peels off over time. Plastic and aluminum rails are available but again cost more. Discourage the use of wrought iron rails for over time maintenance is intensive.

FINISH FLOORING INSTALLATION

Before installing finish flooring check all frame floors for squeaks and loose spots. Remedy the situation using dry wall screws – as many as it takes. Use the proper underlayment for wood, tile, and vinyl flooring. Do tile work first followed by wood flooring and then the vinyl.

When using ceramic tile use marble thresholds under doors or a temporary wooden ground to ensure tile is perfectly straight where it meets a different type of flooring. Be sure the tile man knows which way the doors swing so the marble threshold is directly under the door when closed. When tiling a portion of the floor in a large room, use a temporary wooden ground that the tile man can go up to and leave a perfectly straight line.

Use rosin paper to cover wood and tile floors and then have the cabinets and vanities installed.

TRIM

With interior stonework done, walls painted, trim primed or stained and sealed, permanent flooring and cabinets and vanities installed all trim can be installed.

Trim stairs easily by installing base mold atop the dresser boards the framer used on each side of the stairway. See drawing in Section 9. Box in unsightly beams composed of multiple plys of dimension lumber if not dry walled.

CROWN MOLD AND FALSE BEAMS

False beams can easily be installed on a flat ceiling and at the ridge of vaulted ceilings when drywall tape loosens or cracks. See drawing in Section 9.

If truss uplift results in drywall tape separation where walls meet the ceiling, a two-step ceiling trim attached ONLY to the ceiling and not the wall will cover the gap. Good 1" x 4" boards ripped to produce a 1 ¼" and 2 ¼" wide pieces will suffice. Only on steeper pitched ceilings will the sides of the 1 ¼" wide ripped 1 bys need to be beveled. See drawing in Section 9.

Assemble continuous interior stairway handrails to a good 1 x 8 and secure to wall with screws and finishing washers. Materials should be primed or finished before installing. See drawing in Section 9.

Install finish wood treads and risers on stairway. Do not install locksets or door bumpers.

Save all special tools used on pocket doors, sliding doors, and hinged door locksets for client.

SECTION 5: CONSTRUCTION SEQUENCE

The method of building a house outlined here has been modified little in over 60 years of use by our family construction business. Even when modified to suit a particular situation it produces great results. Continued use brings familiarity and better performance even for commercial projects. The steps involved follow:

1. Call 811 to have all utilities located.
   Apply for power.
   Do survey if required and have flood zone benchmark established if needed.
   Drill well or have water meter installed.
   Notify subcontractors and suppliers.
   Submit truss orders.
   Order job site temporary toilet.

2. Excavate, install culverts, grade out road and drive and then gravel them.
   Install septic and have inspected. After approval of system cover and grade.
   Seed if necessary.
   Set temporary pole; dig trench for wire if service is underground.
   Have temporary pole inspected.
   Then close the ditch.
   Order rebar and rod chairs.

3. Dig footer and place rebar.
   Footing inspection.
   Pour footing.
   Give client selection sheet #1.

4. Form and pour walls or order block, mix, sand, vents, etc.
   Lay block.
   Tie in survey when walls completed.
   Check elevations and dimensions.
   Prepare tie beam.
   Inspection.
   Pour tie beam.

5. Level dirt in crawl space.
   Rough grade dirt for concrete slabs.
   Waterproofing.
   Foundation Drains.
   Gutter Drains.
   Under slab plumbing if necessary.
   Plumbing, waterproofing, and drain inspections.
   Rough grade and backfill.
   Prepare slab.

Termite treatment.
Slab inspection.
Pour slab.
Stucco blockwork if not done by mason after tie beam poured.
Get selection sheet #1 from client.

6. Ready print and material list for framers.
Deliver take off by order to lumber supplier.
Confirm delivery dates for trusses, windows, hinge and glass doors, special beams, pocket and sliding doors.
Order tubs and showers.
Order fireplace.
Order dumpster.

7. Frame.
Order loads as needed.
Use crane for trusses, 2nd story material delivery.
Do all flashing.
Order roofing material and distribute on dried-in roof.
Order metal chimney cap if needed.

8. Client visit to review phone, TV, electric locations, kitchen, and baths.
Give client selection sheets #2

9. Subcontractors in this order: Plumber, Heating Contractor, Electrician, Gas installer.
Be sure any roof penetrations by the above are dried in immediately.
Finish coat on wood fascia.
Check all flashing installations.
Check fire caulking.

10. All inspections.
Roof installation.
Straighten 2x4 and 2x6 walls.
Insulation.
Insulation inspection.
Drywall delivery.
Haul trash off if necessary and return dumpster to jobsite.

11. Install siding (if not completed by framer), soffit, gutters, and gutter guard.
    Install drywall.
    Get all selection sheets #2 from client.
    Give client selection sheet #3.
    Order paint & stain.
    Order cabinets & tops.
    Order garage doors and operators.
    Get selection sheet #3 from client.
    Order trim.

12. Paint and stain.
    Before any finish flooring is installed on frame floors check for loose sheeting and squeaks.
    Install any interior stonework.
    Install any tile floors.
    Install wood floors; cover high traffic areas with resin paper.
    Install vinyl flooring.
    Install cabinets and tops.

13. Install trim.
    Have light fixtures, ceiling fans, appliances, and range hood delivered.
    Install gas appliances and gas tank.
    Install closet shelving.

14. Plumber, Heating Contractor, and Electrician finish their work.
    Electrician hot checks entire electrical system.

15. Painter finishes.
    Install house address numbers.
    Install mailbox if homeowner supplies it.
    Hang doors, adjust and install all door hardware.
    Install shower rods, towel bars, and paper holders.
    Clean entire house.
    Install Screens.
    Haul dumpster away.
    Grade and seed yard.
    Finish gravel drive.
    Have water meter installed.

16. Final inspections and certificate of occupancy.
    Install carpet.
    Vacuum carpet.
    Miscellaneous touch up.
    Have job site toilet picked up.

17. Final walk through checking everything.

SECTION 6: SAMPLE DOCUMENTS

Contract for construction
Specifications
Change order

Builder Name
Address
Phone #
License #

Client Names
Address
Phone #

_____ will construct a residence for you per the accompanying plans and specifications on your lot Pin # _____, in _____, _____ County, NC for the sum of _____ including permit, materials, and labor. Deposit of $ _____ received on _____.
All work will conform to North Carolina and/or _____ County requirements.
Title Insurance is lot owner's obligation.
Monies due _____ are payable by cashier's check in United States currency as follows:

- Deposit $ _____
- Masonry Walls & Footings $ _____
- 2nd Floor Sheeted $ _____
- Roof Dried In $ _____
- Ready For Drywall $ _____
- Trim Completed $ _____
- Upon Final Inspection $ _____

All Payments and any extras are due within 10 days of billing or reaching stage of completion required for any specific draw.
Occupancy will not be granted until all monies have been received by
_____. Its employees and agents are not responsible for any personal items on the premises during the life of this contract.
Costs for changes made after prints are completed and signed begin at $100.00
Homeowner's insurance is to be in effect prior to the Final Inspection and issuance of a Certificate of Occupancy.
Additional Expenses due to blasting of rock or foundation requirements other than standard spread footings and pads will be charges as an extra.
Allowances included in this contract are as follows:

- Flooring Installed and Finished $ _____
- Cabinets & Vanities (including poured tops) installed $ _____
- Fixtures and Fans $ _____
- Appliances $ _____
- Water Line, pump, tank, and wiring installed $ _____
- Interior wood accents installed & finished $ _____
- Wood Stairway installed & finished $ _____
- Front Door purchase allowance $ _____

_____
Client

_____   _____
Client   General Contractor

Specifications

BUILDER:

OWNER:

PROPERTY ADDRESS:

LOT: SUBDIVISION: CITY:

GENERAL: All construction shall equal or exceed the Loaning Institution construction requirements, Local building codes, zoning ordinances and deed restrictions. No materials specified herein shall be substituted except upon agreement of the owner, and the Contractor.
All work shall pass final inspection.

1. METERS: Install 1 Electric meter...in contractors name.
    Deposits made by contractor during construction.

2. LAYOUT: Locate building on site and erect batter boards as required. It shall be the responsibility of the contractor, to verify all setbacks for compliance to zoning ordinances and deed restrictions.

3. EXCAVATION: Top of footing shall be below existing grade at all points except on solid rock

4. CONRETE WORK: Footings to be on reinforced concrete of a minimum 3000 lb. mix. Beams, columns, lintels, and floor slabs to be minimum 3000 lb. mix, reinforced as detailed on plans. All slabs fill or on grade shall be reinforced. All floor slabs on fill under living quarters shall have an approved membrane underneath. All reinforcing steel shall be lapped 40 diameters where spliced.
    Footing size 8" x 20"; Reinforcing: 2-#5 steel rebar.
    Tie Beam Blocks 1 #5 steel rebar.
    Other: Termite Treated Soil

5. MASONRY: Foundation – Concrete block 8" _____ 12" _____ Poured Concrete _____
    Floors – Slab on fill. Reinforcing: Mesh
    All masonry to be of size indicated on plans, laid in mortar mix or cement mortar.

6. FIREPLACE: 1 gas fireplace with gas logs   PREFAB _____   MASONRY _____
    Fireplace Mantel 4x10 Cedar or Pine   Hearth Material: Stone Veneer
    Other: Stone Veneer Hearth & Cheeks to Mantle height.

7. LUMBER: Floor framing MAIN LEVEL: Material: Trusses Grade: Engineered Spacing: 16" O.C.
                          Joists: Size: _____ Grade: _____ Spacing:
             SUBFLOORING – Material: 23/32" Grade: Advantek Size: 4'x8' laid straight
             WALL AND PARTITION FRAMING:
                     Interior Wall Studs - Material: SPF Grade: STUD Size: 2x4 16" O.C.
                     Exterior Wall Studs – Material: SPF Grade: STUD, #2 Size: 2x6 16" O.C.

Sheathing horizontal, 7/16" OSB. Frame houses shall have house wrap under siding.

ROOF FRAMING – Rafters-Material: Trusses   Grade: Engineered   Size: 24" & O.C.
                     Joists: Size: _____   Grade: _____   Spacing: _____
                     Sheathing-Material: 7/16" OSB Solid; Size: 4'x8'
                     Cornice or Eaves – Boxed, vinyl soffit; cedar fascia. Projection: 12"& 16"
                     Ridge vent.

8.   SIDING – Type: Vinyl   Type:

9.   MILLWORK: Wood: Size: Cement: Size:

- Front Door – Type: Insulating Metal   Thickness: 1 ¾"
- Rear Door – Insulating Metal   Thickness: 1 ¾"
- Interior Doors – Type: HC Birch or Masonite 6 panel   Thickness: 1 3/8" & 1"
- Special Doors – Type: Atrium as per print.
- Trim – Size: 2 ¼"   Type: Clear
- Base – Size: 3 ¼"   Type: Clear
- Windows – Ellison Vinyl Double Hung
- Plate mirrors over vanities.
- Clothes Closets & Linen Closet shelving, vinyl wrapped shelving.
- Cabinets – Kitchen – Material: Installed cabinets and vanity allowance including all tops - $ _____
- Garage Doors: Types: Sectional   Size: _____ x _____   Material: Steel (with operators)

10. ROOFING:
        225 lb. Asphalt singles over 30 lb. felt ELK PRETIQUE II
        Metal drip edge should be used on all eaves and rakes of roof.

11. SHEET METAL:
        Flashings – Material: Aluminum, Galvanized
        Valleys – Material: Aluminum
        Gutters and Downspouts – Material: Aluminum Gauge: Standard Residential

12. DRYWALL: ½" Drywall. Standard finishes include: smooth walls, textured ceilings and closet walls.

13. STUCCO: Thickness a minimum of ¼". Exposed block stuccoed, unpainted. Poured walls not stuccoed.

14. WATERPROOFING: Caulk all openings.

15. PAINTING: Exterior Doors – 2 coats of paint.
                     Interior wood work stained _____   Painted _____
                     Fascia stained.
                     Kitchen and bathroom walls to be painted with 2 coats of vinyl acrylic paint.
                     Other walls 2 coats of Vinyl Acrylic
                     Ceilings 0 coats.

16. PRESERVATIVE: All wood coming in contact with masonry walls or concrete floors will be ground contact grade.

17. PLUMBING:
    - Sewage disposal - _____ Bedroom sewer tap fee included. Sewer pipe to be PVC. Septic _____
    - Water supply – Water tap fee included. Pipe for gas. Well _____
    - Water piping – Copper tubing in house. PVC and/or from meter to house.

NUMBER	FIXTURES	MANUFACTURES
	Kitchen Sink	
	Bath Tub	
	Shower	
	Lavatory	
	Water Closet	

Note: It is understood that if any of the above specified fixtures are not available at time of Installation, fixtures of equal grade and quality may be substituted.

    - FAUCETS – Type: Moen
    - SILLCOCKS - Number: 2
    - Accessories – Paper Holder, Towel Bars (No. 1/bath) Material: Composite, Wood, and Metal
        - Allowance: Included

18. ELECTRIC WIRING:
    - Service – underground if applicable and available, Telephone.
    - SWITCHES: Number: As per print & code
    - OUTLETS: Number: As per print & code
    - Power Outlets for Range, Water Heater
    - Other: Dryer, Heat Pump
    - _____ Phone Jacks
    - _____ TV jacks
    - Doorbell: Allowance $ included in fixture allowance

19. ELECTRIC WIRING: Fixture allowance $ _____ Includes door chime and button.

20. HARDWARE: Rough-Furnished as required. Finish Hardware: Included deadbolts exterior locks on hinge doors. Door checks, required on all outward opening exterior doors.

21. GLASS and GLAZING: All window glass to insulated.
    Obscure Locations _____

22. STRUCTURAL STEEL: Reinforcing stell and structural shapes to be installed as shown on drawings.

23. WEATHER STRIPPING: Integral, Metal Thresholds all exterior doors. Material: Aluminum composites.

24. INSULATION: Type: Fiberglass. Roof or ceiling-R-38. Walls-R-19. Floor-R-19.
    Garage Ceiling-R-19. Garage Walls-R-19

25. VINYL FLOORING: See itme 36.

26. EQUIPMENT: Water Heater - Electric, Automatic, Manual. Size - _____. Allowance: Included
Heater-Make: Heat Pump. Seer- _____, Forced air with ducts. Allowance: Included
Air conditioning-Central with ducts,
Includes: Dryer vent; Unvented range hood

27. GRADING: Backfill around all excavations. Grading-Finish. Lawn-Seed.

28. CLEANING: Job shall be left broom clean and all debris removed from under building site.

29. WALKS and DRIVES: As indicated plot plan.
Drives-Width: 16' ±   Thick: 4"   Material: Gravel

30. PERMITS: Building Permits by General Contractor.

31. SOCIAL SECURITY: By Contractor.

32. WORKMEN'S COMPENSATION: By Contractor.

33. BUILDERS RISK and FIRE INSURANCE: By contractor with provisions for contractor and
Owner as Interest may appear.

34. PATENT INFRIGEMENTS: To be defended by contractor.

35. GUARANTEE: Contractor shall guarantee all work for one year, against defective material or
Workmanship.

36. MISCELLANEOUS: Describe any materials or features of constructions not adequately covered
in the drawings or specifications.
    - Appliances-$ _____ allowance (disposal, dishwasher, and microwave)
    - Finish Flooring allowance installed: $ _____
    - No HOA assessments or impact fees included
    - Unpainted pressure treated porch & deck floors, railings, posts, beams & exterior
      steps.
    - Screening porches is NOT included.

37. EXTRAS: No payments will be allowed for any extra work except by order from owner.

38. Plans and Specifications shall be co-operative. Items specified in one but not in the other shall be
include as though covered in both. In case of conflict, specifications shall govern.

THE ABOVE SPECIFICATIONS ARE HEREBY APPROVED:

BY CONTRACTOR _____ **DATE** _____

BY OWNER _____ **DATE** _____

BY OWNER _____ **DATE** _____

26

CHANGE ORDER

Builder Name
Address
Phone #

TO:

Phone:

Date:

Job/Location:

Job Number:

Date of existing contract:

We hereby agree to make the change (s) specified below: **Amount**

Original contract price

Change order #1

This Change Order:

    1.

    2.

New Total

NOTE: This Change Order becomes part of and in conformance with the existing contract.

WE AGREE hereby to make change(s) specified above at this price: $

Date: **Previous Contract Amount** $

Authorized Signature (contractor):   **Revised Contract Total** $

ACCEPTED- The above prices and specifications of this
Change Order are satisfactory and are hereby accepted.   Date of acceptance_____
All work to be performed under same terms and
conditions specified in original contract unless otherwise   Signature_____
stipulated.   **(OWNER)**

Signature_____
(OWNER)

SECTION 7:   MATERIAL ORDER FORMS

Concrete and Masonry
Framing Takeoff
Floor and Exterior Walls
Second Floor
Second Floor Walls
Decks and Roof
Windows and Doors
Siding and Drywall
Trim

Concrete Masonry Takeoff

JOB:

		8"	12"
Big Square for batter boards: **Diagonal:**	X		
Rebar:	#5		
	#3	16" lengths for grade pegs	
Block:			
		8"	12"
	Regular		
	Halves		
	Half High		
	Open Bottom		
	Bond Beam		
	Headers		
CONCRETE:			
	Footing		
	Bond Beam		
	Slab		
	Precast Lintels:		
	Type "S" Mortar Mix:		
	Masons Sand:		
MISC:			
	Rod Chairs:		
	Bar Ties:		
	Wire Mesh:		
	Visqueen:		
	Cavity Caps:		
	4" Expansion Joint:		
	Foundation Vents:		

½" Anchor Bolts (GALV):	For: 1 Tie Beams
Proper length:	2 Garage Door
Jambs	
Proper Washers:	
Water Proofing:	
4" Styrofoam Wrapped Foundation Drains:	
Filter Fabric:	
4" Solid Black Pipe for Gutter Drains:	
4" Fittings-couplings: Y	
T	
90 Bends	

BAGS OF THOROSEAL OR EQUIVALENT.

Framing Takeoff

JOB:

FLOOR:

2x8 PT:

Spruce 2x10:

Spruce 2x12:

¾" T&G plywood-Advantek:

1x3 Stripping:

2x4 PT:

2x4 Spruce:

2x6 Spruce:

Glue (liquid nails):

Shim Shingles:

16D Nails:

8D Nails:

EXTERIOR WALLS:

2x4 Spruce:

2x6 Spruce:

2x8 Spruce:

2x10 Spruce:

2x12 Spruce:

½" 4 ply OSB:

Tyvek:

Hurricane Clips:

Simplex:

Microlam:

2nd Floor

JOB: _____

FLOOR: _____

2x8 PT: _____

Spruce 2x10: _____

Spruce 2x12: _____

¾" T&G plywood-Advantek: _____

1x3 Stripping: _____

2x4 PT: _____

2x4 Spruce: _____

2x6 Spruce: _____

Glue (liquid nails): _____

Shim Shingles: _____

16D Nails: _____

8D Nails: _____

____inch Aluminum Falshing: _____

_____

_____

_____

_____

_____

_____

_____

_____

_____

_____

2nd Floor Walls

JOB:

EXTERIOR WALLS:

2x4 Spruce:

2x6 Spruce:

2x8 Spruce:

2x10 Spruce:

2x12 Spruce:

½" 4 ply OSB:

Tyvek:

Hurricane Clips:

Simplex:

Microlam:

Beams:

6x6 PT:

2x8 PT:

2x10 PT:

2x12PT:

2x4 PT Beam Bottoms:

2x6 PT Beam Bottoms:

Glulam:

Decks & Roof

JOB:

Decks:

2x6 PT Decking:

2x6 PT Joists:

2x8 PT Joists:

2x8 PT Beams:

2x10 PT Beams:

2x12 PT Beams:

2x4 PT Ledger:

16d Galvanized Nails:

Joist Hangers:

ROOF:

½" 4 Ply OSB:

1x3 Stripping:

2x4 Spruce:

2x6 Spruce:

2x6 Spruce Valley Sets:

2x8 Spruce:

2x10 Spruce:

2x12 Spruce:

30# Felt:

Simplex:

Plywood Clips:

Joist Hangers:

Windows and Doors

JOB:

WINDOWS & DOORS:

Atrium Doors:

Glass Doors:

3-0 Hinged Entry:

2-8 Hinged Entry:

1x8 Cedar/Spruce (G.D.Trim):

2-0 x 3-0:

2-0 x 4-0:

3-0 x 3-0:

3-0 x 4-0:

3-0 x 5-0:

4-0 x 2-0:

4-0 x 3-0:

4-0 x 4-0:

1-0 x 5-0:

2-0 x 5-0:

Grilles Between Glass:

Any obscure glass:

INSIDE:

2x4 Spruce:

2x6 Spruce:

Insulation:

Pocket Doors:

Fireplace:

SIDING & DRYWALL

JOB:

SIDING, SOFFIT, FASCIA, RAILS & STEPS:

1x___Wood Siding:

4x___Plywood Siding:

1x12 Cedar Birdboxes:

1x10 Cedar-Garage Door:

1x8 Cedar:

1x6 Cedar-Fascia:

1x4 Cedar:

Brickmold-Garage Door, Glass Door:

3/8" Fir Plywood:

Railings:

     4x4 PT:

     2x4 PT:

     2x2 PT:

Steps:

     2x12 PT:

     2x6 PT-Treads:

     Door Jambs:

Sakrete:

Cement Siding:

ROOF: SHINGLES Squares:

     Starter Bundles:

     Cap-Linear Feet:

     Drip Edge Linear Feet:

     16" Valley Flashing:

     Black Sealant:

     2" Nails:

     Ridge Vent 4':

DRYWALL:

     Garage:

     1st Floor:

     2nd Floor:

TRIM

JOB:

Prehungs:	RH	LH	STYLE
1-6:			
2-0:			
2-4:			
2-6:			
2-8:			
3-0:			
Bifolds:			
1-6:			
2-0:			
2-4:			
2-6:			
2-8:			
3-0:			

Jamb Width:	4 9/16"	6 9/16"	LOCKS:
Doors:			Deadbolt:
1x4 Spruce:			Entry:
Garage:			Bedroom:
Scuttles:			Closet:
1x6 Spruce:			Plates:
Jambs:			Knobs:
Beams:			Pocket Privacy:
1x8 Spruce:			
Beams:			MISCELLANOUS:
Handrails:			Thresholds:
Misc:			Windchain:
1x10 Spruce:			Underlay:
1x12 Spruce:			Door Stop:
Casing-Windows:			Medicine Cabinets:
Casing-Doors:			Pine Panel:
BASE:			Railings:
Oval Handrails:		Handrail Brackets:	
¾" Cove Mold:		Mantle Stock:	

SECTION 8: CLIENT SELECTION SHEETS

Initial Selections #1
Interior Finish #2–1
Interior Finish #2–2
Electrical Fixtures #3

Builder Name

License#   Client:

Phone#   Date:

Initial Selections #1

Job:

Window Color:

     Grilles Between Glass

     Obscure Glass

Master Bath Tub:

Bath #2 Tub:

Bath #3 Tub:

Bath #4 Tub:

Door Styles:

     Front:

     Rear:

     Garage:

Gutter Color:

Shingle Color:

Siding Color:

Soffit Color:

Fascia Color:

Drip Edge Color:

Interior Finish #2-1

Job:

Appliances:

Dishwasher:

Disposal:

Microwave:

Trash Compactor:

Refrigerator:

Washer:

Dryer:

Flooring:

- Carpet:
- Vinyl:
- Wood/Laminate:
- Tile:
- Grout Color:

Interior Doors & Trim:

- Masonite 6 Panel:
- Flush Birch:
- Other (possible upcharge):
- Stain Color (if stained):
- Cabinet Handles (if desired):

Door Hardware Color:

- Hinges & Handles:

Exterior Doors Hardware Color:

Interior Finish #2-2

Job:

Cabinets:

Kitchen:

- Master Bath:
- Bath #2:
- Bath #3:
- Bath #4:
- Powder Room:

Counter Tops:

- Master Bath:
- Bath #2:
- Bath #3:
- Bath #4:
- Powder Room:

Paint Colors:

Inside:

Outside:

- Doors & Jambs:
- Siding:
- Trim:
- GARAGE DOOR(S)

Plumbing:

- Stainless Kitchen Sink:
- Chrome Faucets:
- Special Faucets:

Miscellaneous:

- Stone Veneer Color:
- Switch & Plug Color:
- Glass In Garage Door (may result in upcharge):
- Shelving Wrapped wire shelving, wood will result in upcharge

Electrical Fixtures #3

Job:

Living/Great Room:

Family Room:

Kitchen:

Kitchen Sink:

Master Bedroom:

Bedroom #2:

Bedroom #3:

Bedroom #4:

Master Bath:

Bath #2:

Bath #3:

Bath #4:

Powder Room:

Utility Room:

Dining Room:

Hall:

Hall:

Hall:

Foyer:

Garage (inside):

Garage (outside):

Front Porch:

Rear Porch:

CHIME AND BUTTON:

SECTION 9:   DRAWINGS

Wall Selection
Stairway Geometry
Cross Section
Cross Section
Miscellaneous
Hand Rail and Dresser Board

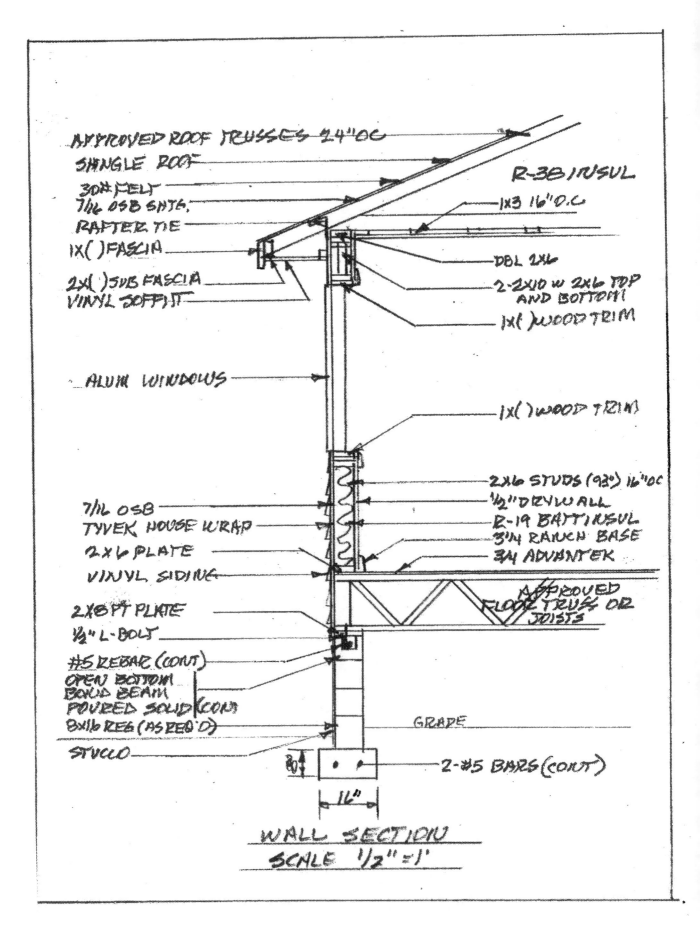

APPROVED ROOF TRUSSES 24" OC
SHINGLE ROOF
30# FELT
7/16 OSB SHTG.
RAFTER TIE
1X( ) FASCIA
2X( ) SUB FASCIA
VINYL SOFFIT

R-38 INSUL
1X3 16" O.C
DBL 2X6
2-2X10 W 2X6 TOP AND BOTTOM
1X( ) WOOD TRIM

ALUM WINDOWS

1X( ) WOOD TRIM

7/16 OSB
TYVEK HOUSE WRAP
2X6 PLATE
VINYL SIDING

2X6 STUDS (92⅝") 16" OC
½" DRYWALL
R-19 BATT INSUL
3¼ RANCH BASE
¾ ADVANTEK

2X8 PT PLATE
½" L-BOLT

APPROVED FLOOR TRUSS OR JOISTS

#5 REBAR (CONT)
OPEN BOTTOM
BOND BEAM
POURED SOLID (CONT)
8X16 REG (AS REQ'D)

GRADE

STUCCO

2-#5 BARS (CONT)

16"

WALL SECTION
SCALE ½" = 1'

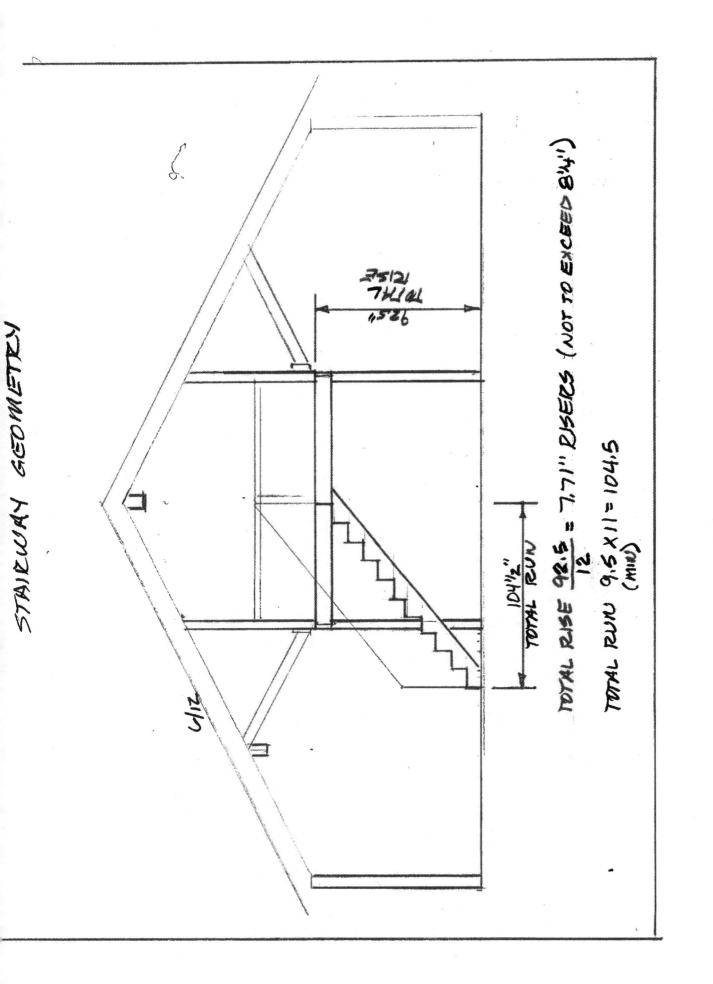

STAIRWAY GEOMETRY

TOTAL RISE $\dfrac{92.5}{12}$ = 7.71" RISERS (NOT TO EXCEED 8'4")

TOTAL RUN 9.5 × 11 = 104.5 (MIN)

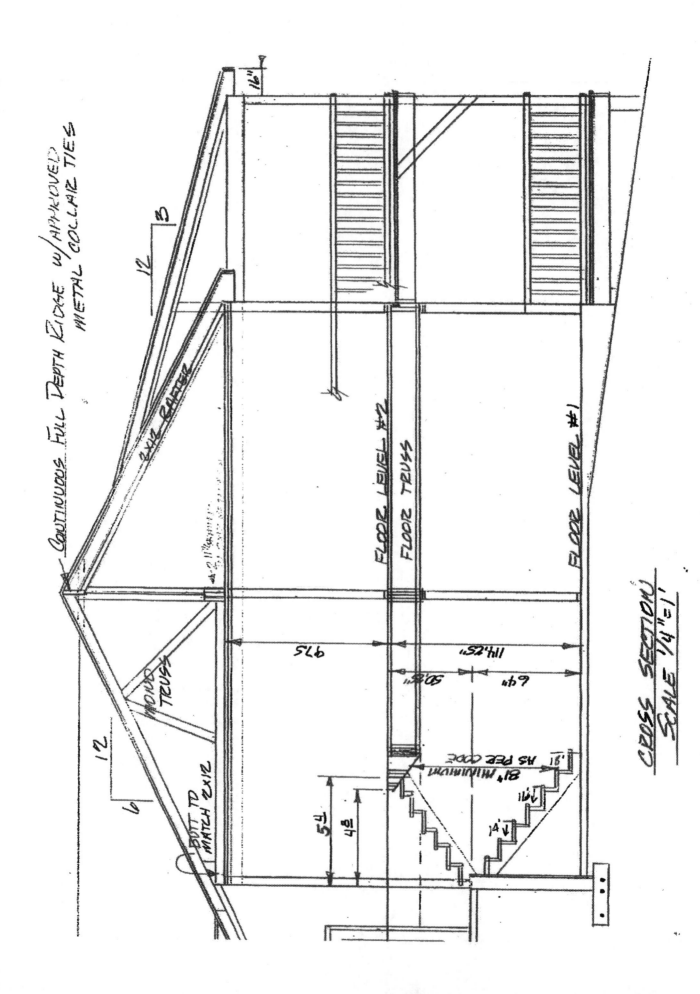

CROSS SECTION
SCALE 1/4"=1'

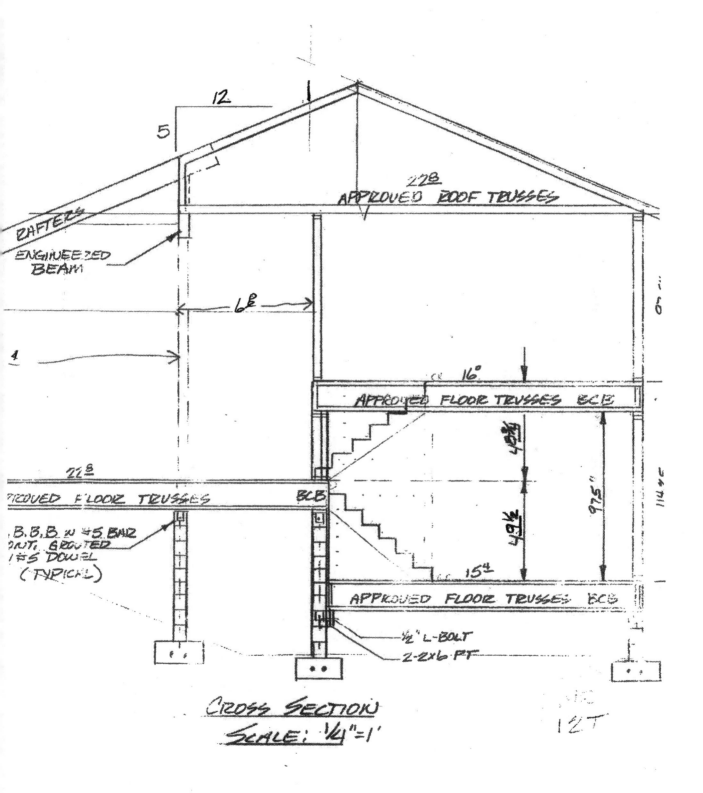

12

5

RAFTERS

ENGINEERED
BEAM

6⅞

4

22⁸
APPROVED ROOF TRUSSES

16"

APPROVED FLOOR TRUSSES BCB

49½

9.75"

114½

6'

22⁸
APPROVED FLOOR TRUSSES   BCB

49½

.B.B.B N #5 BAR
ONT. GROUTED
1#5 DOWEL
(TYPICAL)

15⁴

APPROVED FLOOR TRUSSES BCB

½" L-BOLT
2-2X6 PT

CROSS SECTION
SCALE: ¼"=1'

12T

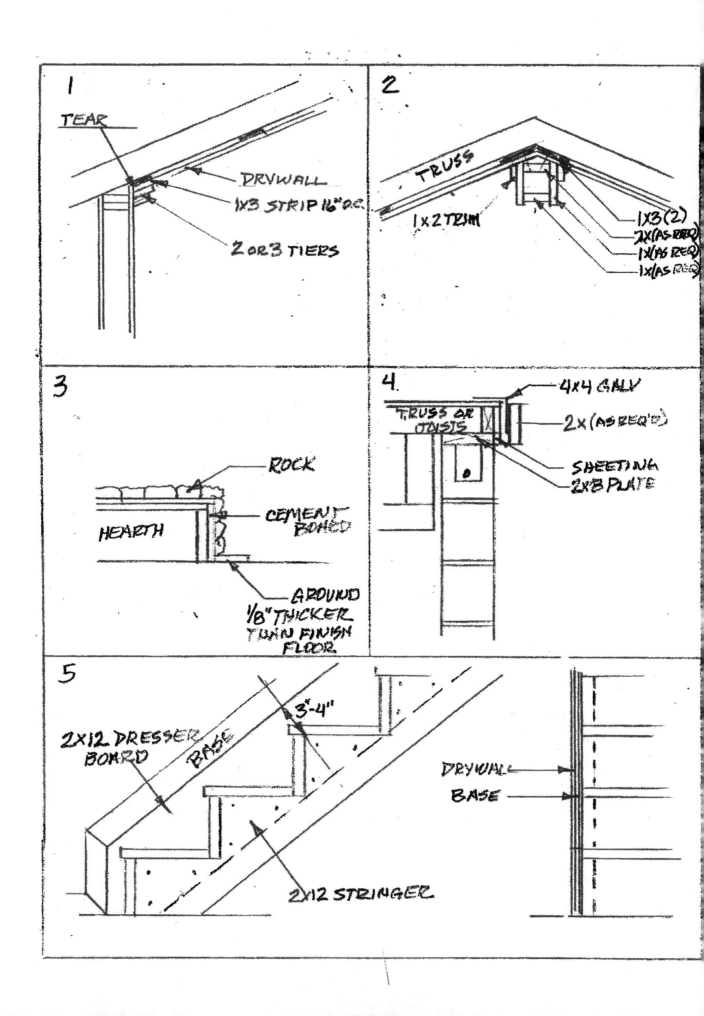

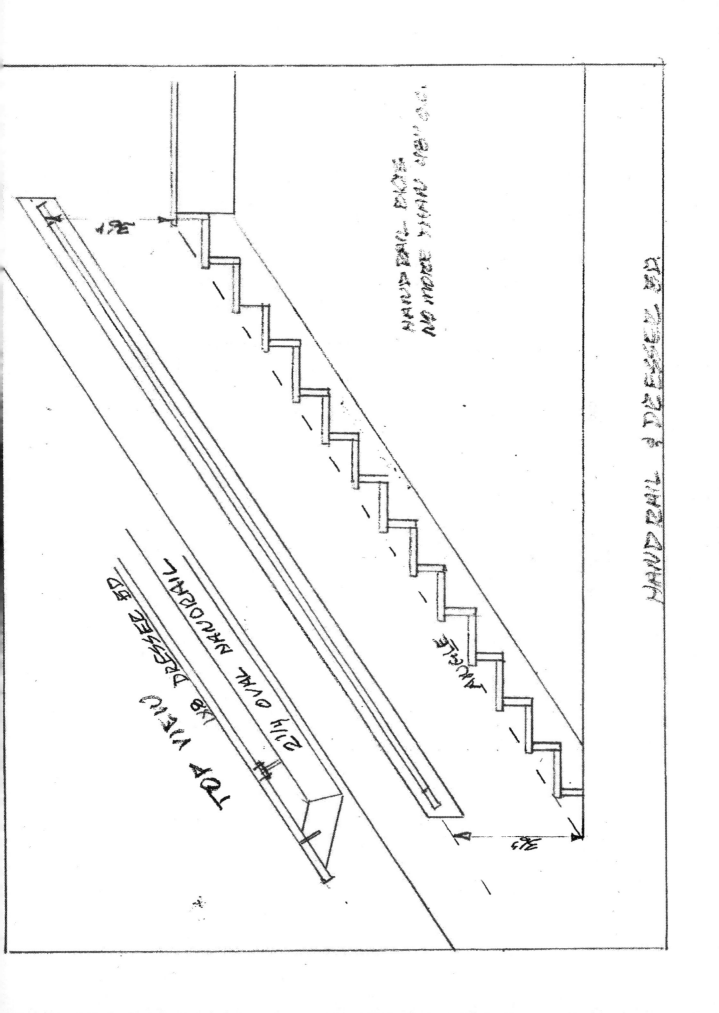

HANDRAIL & DRESSER BD

ABOUT THE AUTHOR

Ron Benhart

I have been married for 60 years to my wife and rock, Rebecca. Together we have 3 daughters. In 1958 my family moved from Illinois to Florida. I worked in the family construction business part time from 1952-1960.

I attended St. Petersburg Junior College, from 1958-1960. I then attended and graduated from the University of Florida, 1960-1962, where I majored in Forest Management. I was a practicing Forester from 1962-1971.

I rejoined the Family Construction Business in 1971, obtaining my Florida Building License in 1975 and became the Family Construction Business President in 1976. In 1989 I obtained my North Carolina Contractor License. I have been retired from the construction business since 2019, but I still maintain an active license.

Printed in the United States
By Bookmasters